For
My Son

For My Son

{ special memories
of our life together }

AARP

LARK BOOKS
A Division of Sterling Publishing Co., Inc.
New York / London

Dedicated with love,
to my wonderful daughter
Corrina

Text:
Deborah Morgenthal

Book design & illustrations:
susanmcbridedesign.com

Editorial assistance:
Mark Bloom

Production assistance:
Shannon Yokeley

Cover design:
Susan McBride & Celia Naranjo

AARP Books publishes a wide range
of titles on health, personal finance,
lifestyle, and other subjects that
promise to enrich the lives of
Americans 50+. For more information,
go to www.aarp.org/books.

AARP, established in 1958, is a
nonprofit, nonpartisan organization
with more than 40 million members
age 50 and older. The AARP name and
logo are registered trademarks of AARP,
used under license to Sterling
Publishing Co., Inc.

The recommendations and opinions
expressed herein are those of the
author and do not necessarily reflect
the views of AARP.

Library of Congress Cataloging-in-Publication Data

Morgenthal, Deborah, 1950-
  For my son : special memories of our life together / Deborah Morgenthal. -- 1st ed.
    p. cm.
  Includes index.
  ISBN 978-1-60059-503-5 (hc-trade cloth : alk. paper)
  1. Baby books. 2. Sons. I. Title.
  HQ779.M673 2010
  306.874--dc22

                                        2009030529

10 9 8 7 6 5 4 3 2 1

First Edition

Published by Lark Books, A Division of
Sterling Publishing Co., Inc.
387 Park Avenue South, New York, NY 10016

Text © 2010, Lark Books, A Division of Sterling Publishing Co., Inc.
Illustrations © 2010, Susan McBride

Distributed in Canada by Sterling Publishing,
c/o Canadian Manda Group, 165 Dufferin Street
Toronto, Ontario, Canada M6K 3H6

Distributed in the United Kingdom by GMC Distribution Services,
Castle Place, 166 High Street, Lewes, East Sussex, England BN7 1XU

Distributed in Australia by Capricorn Link (Australia) Pty Ltd.,
P.O. Box 704, Windsor, NSW 2756 Australia

If you have questions or comments about this book, please contact:
Lark Books
67 Broadway
Asheville, NC 28801
828-253-0467

Manufactured in China

ISBN 13: 978-1-60059-503-5

For information about custom editions, special sales, premium and corporate purchases,
please contact Sterling Special Sales Department at 800-805-5489 or specialsales@sterlingpub.com.

With love for:

_____

From:

_____

Date:

_____

contents

Introduction

amilies come in many different shapes and sizes. What time kids go to bed, where meals are eaten, and how much is too much TV are a few of the variables. In some families, children are raised by two adults, and in others by one. Six children feels just right for the Smith's, while three is perfect for the Cohen's. But there's a lot of common ground. Those of us who have had the privilege of raising a child would probably agree that:

We love our children always and forever.

We want the best for them and try to help them realize their full potential.

We make mistakes, even when we try our hardest.

We're delighted by all they learn and teach us.

We're often frustrated by the challenges.

We look forward to the next stage of their lives…and find ourselves missing what's gone.

Then suddenly our nest is empty. Perhaps we wish we'd been more fully present during the short time our kids were in our care. We pour over photo albums, rummage through boxes filled with letters, drawings, and objects that hold meaning, and breathe in the nuanced, spicy aroma of the past. Nothing can bring back those years, but savoring the details of so many small and large events in our child's life helps us remember.

I became a first-time mother at the age of 42 by walking through the door marked "Adoption." Corrina was 32 days old when my husband and I brought her home. We took turns driving so we could sit in the back and look into the sleeping face of our cherub. Now Corrina is 17, gliding and stumbling into her adult life. And here I am, studying old photos and memorabilia to keep her close.

I never filled out a baby book where you could record statistics about baby's height and weight, the names and dates of vaccinations, the many "firsts." Truthfully, I think I felt overwhelmed by the responsibilities of working full-time and trying to raise a healthy and, I hoped, happy child. But now that I'm a card-carrying AARP member, I'm ready to fill one out. I'd like to write down milestones and memories of not just Corrina's first year but of all 17 years. I may have forgotten specific events, but I'm sure that certain things about my daughter's life are filed in my head and heart and just need a bit of prompting to come flooding back.

And I know I'm not alone. When I talked with friends who are also older parents, they expressed an interest in just such a book, too. We agreed that it would invite us to remember and celebrate our son or daughter at three months, three years, and right now, so we could honor that relationship as it continues to unfold. It would encourage us to reflect on what being a parent has taught us. We'd fill the book with words and photos and give it to our young adult on his or her 21st or 30th birthday and say, "Here, honey. I've captured some of you and me in this book. It's filled with pride and love, some insights… and a little mischief."

So that's what I set out to do, and I hope it works for you! The book is organized into eight sections, starting with infancy and traveling towards adulthood. I've devised prompts that helped jump-start my memories at each stage, and perhaps they'll help you, too.

"The first time I held you in my arms, I remember…"

"The nickname you most deserved was…"

"I was so proud of you when…"

"The strangest thing I found under your bed was…"

"I'm touched that you have grown up to be…"

"If I could redo those years as a parent, I'd be sure to…"

You don't have to respond to every prompt. When in doubt, paste in a photo of your son, or a drawing he created. Each section ends with two blank pages in case you need more room for stories and photos. You can enjoy this book if you're the mom or the dad. You raised that son and you have the scars and the kisses to prove it.

In fact, one of the satisfactions of working with this book is that in remembering your son over the years, you'll reacquaint yourself with the parent you were and the parent you've become—and relive how the amazing process of raising a child has changed you and shaped your life.

Don't wait. Start using the book right away. You can work chronologically or skip around through the years. Make copies of photos, ephemera, and artwork to paste in. Someday, on a special birthday, graduation, or celebration, you'll have the perfect gift for your son—filled with love and remembrance.

—Deborah Morgenthal

10

The First Year

Birth to 12 months

When I learned I was going to
be a parent, I

_____

_____

_____

_____

_____

I got ready for your arrival by

_____

_____

_____

_____

_____

_____

_____

12

The first person I told about
you coming into my life was

_____

Your arrival

Where
....

Date   Time
....

Weight   Height
....

You were almost stuck with
the following names

_____
_____
_____
_____
_____

You got the name you did because

_____
_____
_____
_____
_____
_____

The first time I held
you, I remember
thinking

_____
_____
_____
_____
_____
_____
_____
_____

The First Year

13

You were fascinated by

_____

_____

_____

_____

_____

Favorite Music

When you were fussy, I calmed you down by

_____

_____

_____

_____

_____

_____

_____

_____

14

Your much-loved cuddly thing was a

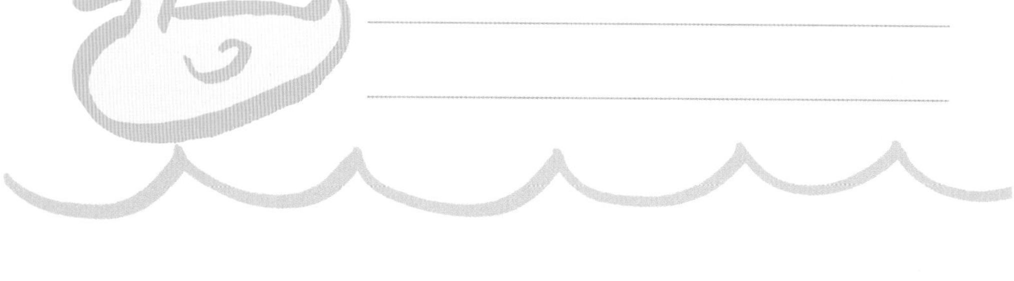

_____

_____

_____

_____

Firsts

Tooth
....

Feeding yourself
....

Crawling
....

Steps
....

Haircut
....

Airplane ride
....

Solid food
....

Word
....

Standing up
....

Slept through the night
....

Long trip
....

Before you could talk, you made some wonderful sounds. I especially loved

_____

_____

_____

_____

_____

_____

_____

The First Year

My favorite way to spend time with you was to

_____

_____

_____

_____

_____

_____

_____

_____

When you could move around on your own, you liked to

_____

_____

_____

_____

_____

_____

_____

_____

Favorite Foods

You refused to eat

I never got tired of watching you

Some baby games we played together were

The First Year

17

You were crabbiest when you

_____

_____

_____

_____

_____

You were most happy when you

_____

_____

_____

_____

_____

Favorite Toys

My pet names for you were

....

....

....

Here's what your brother/sister/
grandma/grandpa called you

_____

_____

_____

_____

_____

19

We celebrated your first birthday by

_____

_____

_____

_____

Here's who shared that special day with you

_____

_____

_____

_____

The First Year

The best thing about
you as a baby was that

_____

_____

_____

_____

_____

_____

_____

_____

_____

_____

_____

20

The scariest moment I had as a new parent was when

. . . .

. . . .

. . . .

. . . .

. . . .

. . . .

. . . .

The most challenging thing
about you as a baby was

_____

_____

_____

_____

_____

_____

_____

_____

_____

_____

I learned so much about myself as a new parent
that first year, such as

_____

_____

_____

_____

_____

_____

_____

If I could redo that first year as a parent, I'd be sure to

_____

_____

_____

_____

_____

The First Year

21

The First Year

Use this space to add more stories and photos.

22

Toddler Time

12 months to 3 years

The nickname you most deserved was

· ·

· ·

The funniest thing you did was

Favorite Foods

26

You absolutely, positively would not
eat the following foods

_____

_____

_____

_____

_____

You were happiest when

_____

_____

_____

_____

_____

_____

_____

Toddler Time

If you could have painted the world one color, it would have been

· ·

So many things captured your
interest, especially

_____

_____

_____

_____

_____

_____

_____

 One of the funny faces you made was

· ·

Your laugh sounded to me like

_____

Here's how I'd describe your toddler self, using each of the letters in that word, as in *"D is for delightful."*

T
....

O
....

D
....

D
....

L
....

E
....

R
....

Toddler Time

You were very proud of yourself when

_____
_____
_____
_____
_____
_____
_____
_____
_____

30

Favorite Toys

Here's what I most liked about you

_____
_____
_____
_____
_____
_____
_____
_____
_____
_____
_____
_____

You had the cutest way of saying certain words and expressions,
for example

Favorite Nursery Rhymes

First thing in the morning you liked to

31

Your bedtime rituals included

Toddler Time

Your most memorable meltdown was

_____

_____

_____

_____

_____

_____

_____

Here are a few choice words that
describe you on a "bad day"

· ·

· ·

· ·

· ·

32

My favorite way to spend time with
you was

_____

_____

_____

_____

_____

_____

You were fearless about

_____
_____
_____
_____
_____
_____
_____

You were afraid of

· ·
· ·
· ·
· ·
· ·
· ·
· ·
· ·
· ·

33

I really understood you were no longer a "baby" when you

_____
_____
_____
_____
_____
_____
_____

Toddler Time

34

The biggest wish I had for you was

_____
_____
_____
_____
_____
_____
_____
_____
_____

Other family members you adored were

_____
_____
_____
_____
_____
_____
_____
_____
_____

We created some family traditions at this time, including

If I could redo those years as a parent, I'd be sure to

Toddler Time

Toddler Time

Use this space to add more stories and photos.

••

Preschool Years

Ages 3 to 6

You loved to pretend that

_____

_____

_____

_____

_____

_____

_____

_____

_____

_____

40

Here's what I most liked about you

_____

_____

_____

_____

_____

_____

_____

_____

_____

You called your imaginary friend

Favorite Books

· ·

· ·

· ·

· ·

When your friends came over to play, you

_____

_____

_____

_____

_____

_____

_____

_____

The biggest mischief you got into was

_____

_____

_____

_____

_____

_____

_____

_____

_____

_____

_____

_____

41

Preschool Years

Your favorite Halloween costume was

_____

_____

_____

_____

_____

You had lots of ways you showed me how much you loved me. Some of the special ones were

_____

_____

_____

_____

_____

You liked to help me

_____

_____

_____

_____

_____

_____

Favorite Clothes

_____

_____

_____

_____

_____

I knew you were growing up when you
insisted on doing this "all by myself"

_____

_____

_____

_____

_____

_____

On a scale of 1 – 10, with 10 being
"I will not share, never, ever," I'd rate you a

1   2   3   4   5   6   7   8   9   10

You had lots of dreams of what you'd be when you
grew up, such as

43

Preschool Years

Favorite Music

. . . .

. . . .

. . . .

. . . .

44

At preschool, you loved to

_____

_____

_____

_____

Your teachers were impressed that you

_____

_____

_____

_____

_____

I hereby award

_____

Best at

_____

_____

_____

Here's your name with all the letters beginning a word that
describes you at this time, as in
"C is because you are courageous."

LETTER   BECAUSE YOU ARE

Preschool Years

Favorite Movies

You were really good at

_____

_____

_____

_____

_____

_____

_____

46

One of the things that
made you feel "big" was

_____

_____

_____

_____

There were lots of things just the two of us
did together, like

_____

_____

_____

_____

_____

With other members of the family you liked to

_____

_____

_____

_____

_____

*Read me the story about
the moon again!
Please, please, please...*

The one story/song/food/outfit that made me want to say—
"Not one more time, please!"

_____

_____

_____

Before you went to bed, you insisted on

_____

_____

_____

_____

Preschool Years

Sometimes we did not see eye to eye, for example

_____

_____

_____

_____

_____

Favorite Foods

· ·

· ·

· ·

· ·

On your list of Most Yucky Foods were

_____

_____

_____

_____

_____

_____

_____

_____

_____

To calm ourselves down, we often

_____

_____

_____

_____

_____

I was so proud of you when

_____

_____

_____

_____

_____

_____

_____

Thank you for showing me how to

_____

_____

_____

_____

_____

_____

_____

_____

If I could redo those years as a parent,
I'd be sure to

_____

_____

_____

_____

_____

_____

_____

_____

Preschool Years

Preschool Years

Use this space to add more photos or stories.

50

52

Primary School Years

Ages 6 to 10

On your first day of school, you were surprised that

_____

_____

_____

_____

_____

54

I was really proud of you for

_____

_____

_____

_____

_____

Favorite School Subjects

_____

_____

You made new friends the first year of school, including

_____

_____

_____

_____

_____

_____

_____

_____

_____

_____

Here are some of the things you really liked
about elementary school

_____

_____

_____

_____

_____

_____

_____

_____

_____

_____

The elementary school subjects you
did the best in were

_____

_____

_____

The things you found challenging about school were

_____

_____

_____

_____

_____

_____

_____

_____

_____

_____

Your favorite activities in school were

. . . .

. . . .

. . . .

. . . .

. . . .

Primary School Years

You were so proud of yourself when you learned to

· ·

· ·

· ·

· ·

When you were with your friends after
school, you always wanted to

Favorite Sport

56

The strangest thing I found under your bed was

In the summer, you really liked doing
these activities

_____

_____

_____

_____

_____

Your favorite family trips were

_____

_____

_____

_____

I remember a lot of handmade
gifts you made for me, including

. . . .

. . . .

You were really good at

. . . .

_____

_____

. . . .

Primary School Years

The family members you most loved hanging out with were

_____

_____

_____

_____

When you didn't feel well, I pampered you by

_____

_____

_____

I could tell you were growing up when you

_____

_____

_____

_____

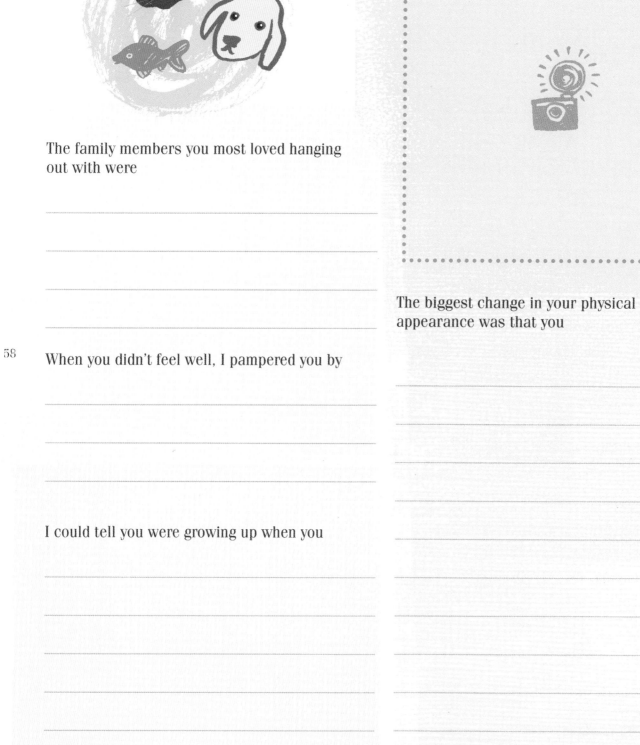

The biggest change in your physical appearance was that you

_____

_____

_____

_____

_____

_____

_____

_____

You said your best birthday "ever" was when

_____

_____

_____

_____

_____

_____

_____

Here's what I most liked about you

_____

_____

_____

_____

_____

_____

You were changing so fast. I couldn't believe that you

· ·

59

· ·

· ·

· ·

Of all the magical characters you believed in back then (such as The Tooth Fairy), you were most disappointed to stop believing in

Primary School Years

· ·

Favorite Movies

. . . .

. . . .

. . . .

. . . .

You were happiest when you

_____

_____

_____

_____

I was so impressed by how much
you knew about

_____

_____

_____

_____

_____

Thinking about you during these years,
I wonder if I shouldn't have named you

_____

_____

_____

_____

_____

_____

_____

_____

_____

If I'd written a chapter book about your life, some of the chapter titles could have been

Age 6:

....

Age 7:

....

Age 8:

....

Age 9:

....

Age 10:

....

There were some scary times over these years, like when you

_____

_____

_____

_____

How did I know you loved me? Here are some of the ways…

_____

_____

_____

_____

If I could redo those years as a parent, I'd be sure to

_____

_____

_____

_____

Primary School Years

Primary School Years

Use this space to add more stories and photos.

62

The Tween Years

Ages 10 to 13

Here's a pie chart showing how you spent your time—using a cell phone, doing homework, talking to friends, etc.

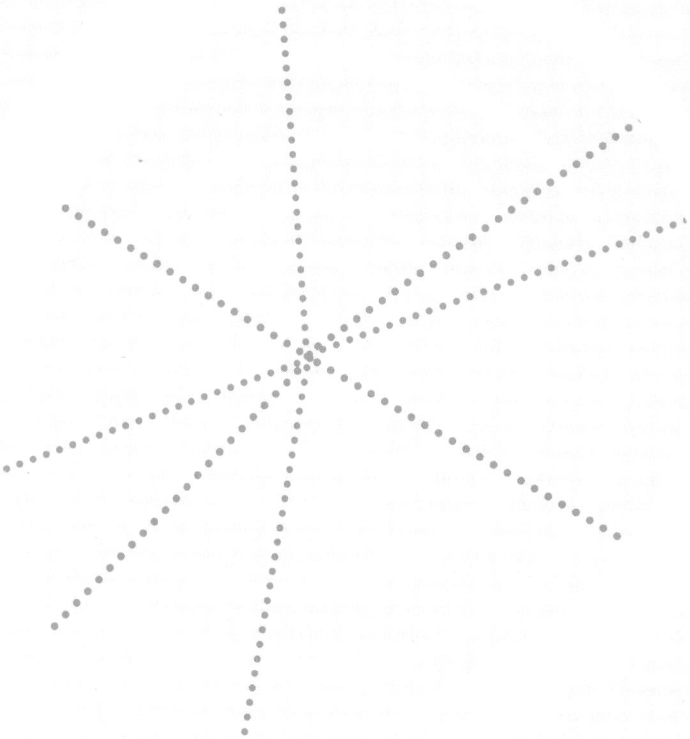

Your best friends were

Favorite Music

You thought certain famous people were very cool. Your Top Ten Cool People list would have included

1
....

2
....

3
....

4
....

5
....

6
....

7
....

8
....

9
....

10
....

In dress and attitude, you imitated certain celebrities, such as

_____

_____

_____

_____

_____

If you'd been the star of a movie, your character would have

_____

_____

_____

_____

The Tween Years

Your best subjects in school were

_____

_____

_____

_____

_____

Favorite Books

· · · · · · · · · · · · · · · · · · · ·

· · · · · · · · · · · · · · · · · · · ·

68

· · · · · · · · · · · · · · · · · · · ·

The things that bugged you the most about school were

_____

_____

_____

_____

_____

_____

Although it was a struggle at times, you really went the distance when you

_____

_____

_____

_____

_____

_____

_____

_____

_____

_____

You were so proud of yourself when

· · · · · · · · · · · · · · · · · · · ·

· · · · · · · · · · · · · · · · · · · ·

· · · · · · · · · · · · · · · · · · · ·

· · · · · · · · · · · · · · · · · · · ·

· · · · · · · · · · · · · · · · · · · ·

· · · · · · · · · · · · · · · · · · · ·

· · · · · · · · · · · · · · · · · · · ·

In the summer, you really loved to

_____

_____

_____

_____

The family vacation you would have repeated again was

_____

_____

_____

_____

_____

_____

_____

_____

_____

If a genie had given you three wishes, you would have wished for

....

....

....

....

....

The Tween Years

Becoming a teenager was a big deal to
you because

_____

_____

_____

_____

_____

_____

_____

_____

The biggest compliment I could give you
was that

_____

_____

I was so proud of you when

_____

_____

_____

_____

_____

Favorite
Sport

Here's what I most liked about you

_____
_____
_____

The most creative way you got into trouble
was when

_____
_____
_____
_____
_____
_____

The one thing I always nagged you about was

_____
_____
_____
_____
_____

71

I embarrassed you the most when

....
....
....
....

The Tween Years

While trying hard to be grown up, you couldn't leave this one childish thing behind

_____

_____

_____

72

_____

In certain ways, you did become more responsible, like when you

_____

_____

_____

_____

_____

_____

Favorite TV Program

. . . .

. . . .

. . . .

. . . .

We had a lot of fun together when we

_____

_____

_____

_____

_____

_____

Some of your favorite words and expressions were

You were interested in learning a lot of new things, such as

73

If I could redo those years as a parent, I'd be sure to

The Tween Years

The Tween Years

Use this space to add more stories and photos.

75

Early Teen Years

Ages 13 to 16

The things you liked best about school were

_____

_____

_____

_____

_____

_____

_____

_____

_____

_____

_____

You took on some new challenges in school, including

_____

_____

_____

_____

You were super proud of yourself when

_____

_____

_____

_____

78

When school was over each day, you were eager to

· ·

· ·

· ·

· ·

· ·

A scorecard of your special interests would have looked like this:

ACTIVITY   COMMENTS

....

....

....

....

....

....

....

....

79

Early Teen Years

Your best friends were

_____

_____

_____

_____

_____

_____

Favorite TV Program

· ·

· ·

· ·

· ·

80

Some of the big adventures you had (that I knew about!) were

_____

_____

_____

_____

_____

_____

_____

The most memorable **"You did what?"** moment for me was when you

_____

_____

_____

_____

Here are several choice words that describe your room

_____

_____

_____

_____

_____

When we disagreed about something, the topic was usually

_____

_____

_____

_____

81

One of your unusual talents that other people didn't know about was

. . . .

. . . .

. . . .

. . . .

Early Teen Years

There were many things I wondered about but never asked, for instance

Your most important accomplishment was

I knew you were leaving childhood behind when you

If you'd been asked to pack one box with the stuff that was special to you, it would have included

82

You were convinced you'd grow up to be a

I was so proud of you when

83

Early Teen Years

Here's what I most liked about you

_____
_____
_____
_____
_____
_____
_____
_____
_____
_____
_____
_____
_____
_____
_____
_____

Favorite Clothes

Favorite Music

I admired the passion you had for

_____

_____

_____

_____

_____

_____

_____

If I could redo those years as a parent, I'd be sure to

_____

_____

_____

_____

Early Teen Years

Early Teen Years

Use this space to add more stories and photos.

Older Teen Years

Ages 16 to 19

And the winner is...Best High School Moments

_____

_____

_____

_____

90

_____

_____

_____

_____

Some of the things you loved about high school were

_____

_____

_____

_____

_____

And there were things that drove you crazy about high school, such as

_____

_____

_____

_____

_____

Favorite Books

. . . .

. . . .

. . . .

. . . .

. . . .

Here's your report card for Typical Teenager Stuff.

A = All the Time and D = Duh, like Never.

	GRADE	COMMENTS
using your cell phone		
staying on the computer		
doing household chores		
watching TV		
hanging out with friends		
cleaning your room		
listening to music		
begging to use the car		
focusing on your physical appearance		
sleeping late on weekends		
working at a part-time job		
finishing all your schoolwork on time		
saving money		
spending money		
doing community volunteer work		
raiding the refrigerator		
reading books		
going to the movies		
playing sports		
watching sports on TV		

Older Teen Years

You were happiest when you

_____
_____
_____
_____
_____
_____
_____

What I thought (and never said) about your first serious romance

· ·
· ·
· ·
· ·
· ·
· ·

I voted ✓

I was really proud of you when

_____
_____
_____
_____
_____
_____

Your closest friends were

_____
_____
_____
_____
_____
_____
_____

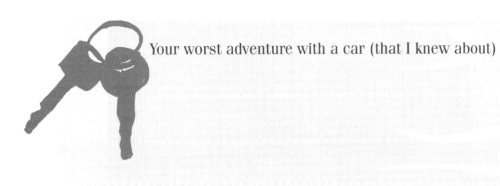

Your worst adventure with a car (that I knew about)

One activity you and I enjoyed together was

_____
_____
_____
_____
_____
_____

_____
_____
_____
_____

I was off-the-charts mad at you the time you

_____
_____
_____
_____
_____
_____

_____
_____
_____
_____

93

Favorite Music

· ·

· ·

· ·

· ·

Older Teen Years

Here's what I most liked about you

_____

_____

_____

_____

_____

_____

_____

_____

You were really good at

_____

Favorite activity

_____

_____

94

_____

_____

_____

_____

_____

_____

The summer and afterschool jobs you enjoyed the most were

_____

_____

_____

_____

_____

One of the secrets you shared with me was

. . . .

. . . .

. . . .

Here are a few of the things I knew about
(that you didn't know I knew)

. . . .

. . . .

. . . .

I first glimpsed the adult you'd
turn out to be when

_____

_____

_____

_____

_____

_____

_____

95

You changed my attitudes about

_____

_____

_____

_____

_____

_____

Older Teen Years

Favorite
TV
Program . . . .

. . . .

I never got tired of watching you

_____

_____

_____

_____

_____

You made a difference in someone's life by

_____

_____

_____

_____

_____

I was very impressed by the way you

_____

_____

_____

_____

_____

_____

_____

_____

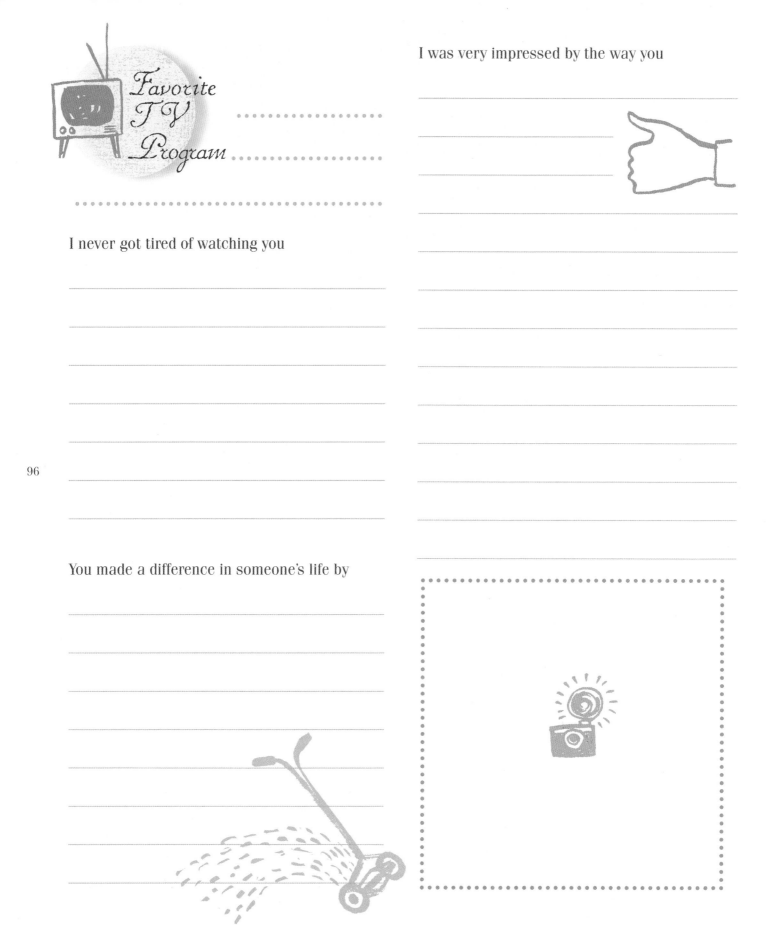

The biggest (and best!) change I saw in you was

_____
_____
_____
_____
_____
_____
_____
_____
_____
_____

Your big dream for yourself was

_____
_____
_____
_____
_____

My big dream for you was

97

_____
_____
_____
_____

If I could redo those years as a parent, I'd be sure to

_____
_____
_____
_____
_____

Older Teen Years

Older Teen Years

Use this space to add more stories and photos.

Young Adult

Age 19+

After high school, you were so ready to

_____

_____

_____

_____

_____

_____

_____

102

_____

_____

_____

College is/was really good for you
because

_____

_____

_____

_____

_____

The big surprise for you
about college is/was

Now you have the skills to pursue the passions
you've always had, for instance

_____

_____

_____

_____

PASSPORT

Here's what I thought (but never said!)
about your first dorm room or apartment

_____

_____

_____

_____

_____

_____

_____

This is what I thought (but never said!)
about your first roommate

· ·

· ·

· ·

· ·

103

You really liked your first "real" job because

_____

_____

_____

_____

Young Adult

I can hardly believe it, but you've finally
learned to

_____

_____

_____

_____

_____

_____

_____

104

*Favorite
Movies*

_____

Here's what I like the best about you

_____

_____

_____

_____

_____

You're happiest when you

_____

_____

_____

_____

_____

_____

We finally agree about

. . . .

. . . .

. . . .

. . . .

You can still brighten my day when you

You're very proud that you have

105

I'm very proud that you have

Young Adult

Here's your name with all the letters beginning a word that describes you at this time, as in *"C is because you are courageous."*

LETTER   BECAUSE YOU ARE

. . . .

. . . .

. . . .

. . . .

. . . .

. . . .

106

. . . .

. . . .

. . . .

. . . .

. . . .

. . . .

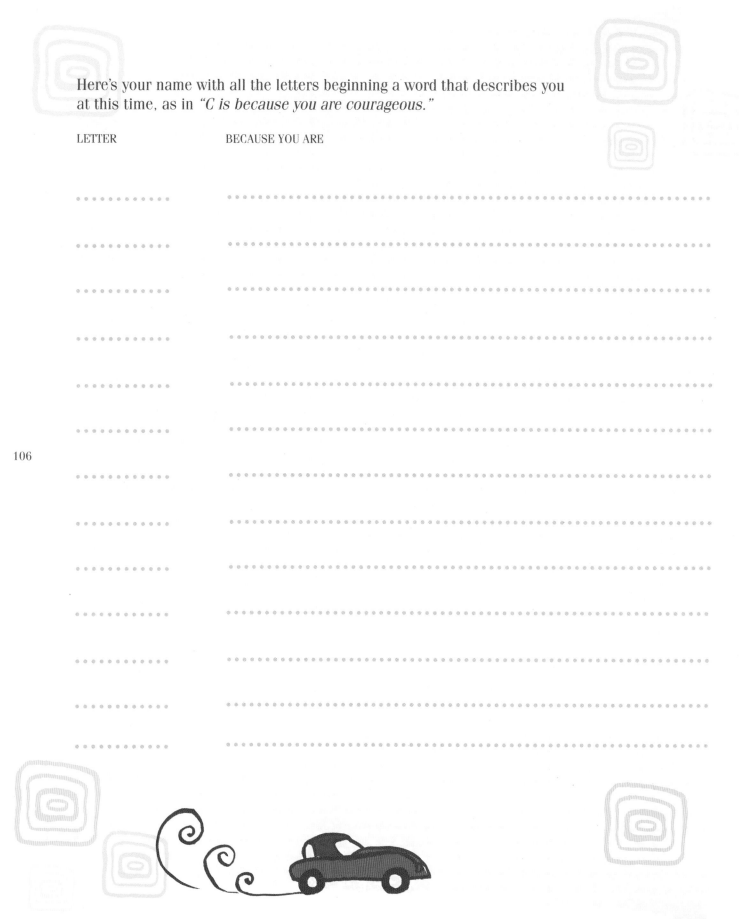

You've changed in so many ways over the years.
But I like that I can still see the toddler, the child,
and the teenager in you. You're still

_____

_____

_____

_____

But you've changed in many important ways, too.
For instance, now you

_____

_____

_____

_____

_____

_____

_____

_____

Favorite activity

_____

_____

_____

_____

_____

_____

Young Adult

I'm touched that you've grown up to be

....

....

....

....

I'm still so impressed that you

The best thing about the two of us getting to be friends as adults is that

108

You and I share some deep values and beliefs, including

....

....

....

....

When we talk about the future, your big dream is

....

....

You've taught me many lessons, especially

If I could wish you one gift for the rest of your life, it would be

109

Young Adult

Young Adult

Use this space to add more stories and photos.

110

Siberian tiger

PHOTO CREDITS

David J. Maenza—Cover

Lynn M. Stone—2, 4 (top), 11 (2 photos), 14, 16 (top) 21 (top left, bottom left, and right), 23 (bottom), 27, 28 (bottom left), 30 (top), 34, 40 (middle and bottom), 42 (top)

Mark Rosenthal—4 (bottom), 12

Tony Freeman—6, 42 (bottom right)

James P. Rowan—8, 13, 16 (bottom), 19, 23 (top), 24 (2 photos), 26, 28 (top, bottom right), 30 (bottom), 33, 35, 36 (2 photos, at right), 38 (top), 40 (top), 42 (bottom left), 44 (3 photos)

Jerry Hennen—21 (top right)

Root Resources—© Anthony Mercieca, 32

Allan Roberts—36 (top, left), 38 (bottom)

COVER—A view of Lincoln Park Zoo, Chicago

Library of Congress Cataloging in Publication Data

Jacobsen, Karen.
    Zoos.

    (A New true book)
    Summary: An introduction to zoos and the
animals that live in them, including the
elephant, rhinoceros, giraffe, antelope,
lion and giant panda.
    1. Zoo animals—Juvenile literature.
2. Zoological gardens — Juvenile
literature.
[1. Zoo animals. 2. Zoological gardens]
I. Title.
QL77.5.J3   1982   590'.74'4   82-9545
ISBN 0-516-01664-4   AACR2